# WABI SABI

## STYLE

# WABI SABI

## S T Y L E

J A M E S   A N D   S A N D R A   C R O W L E Y

*Primary photographer*
J O S E P H   P U T N A M

S A L T   L A K E   C I T Y

First Edition

05 04 03 02 01 5 4 3 2 1



Published by
Gibbs Smith, Publisher
P.O. Box 667
Layton, Utah 84041

Orders: (1-800) 748-5439
www.gibbs-smith.com

Edited by Gail Yngve

Designed by
Kinde Nebeker Design

Printed and bound
in Hong Kong

Library of Congress Cataloging-in-Publication Data

Crowley, James, 1959–

Wabi Sabi style / by James and Sandra Crowley ; primary photographer
Joseph Putnam.— 1st ed.

p. cm.

ISBN 1-58685-010-5 (alk. paper)

1. Design—Japan. I. Crowley, Sandra. 1960– II. Putnam, Joseph.
III. Title.

NK1484.A1 C76 2001

745.4'4952–dc21

00–012129

In memory of
David and Chris

A TRIO OF EIGHTEENTH-CENTURY *MANEKI NEKO*, OR BECKONING CATS, BEAR THE BURDEN OF THEIR AGE WITH GRACE AND CHARM. THESE FRIENDLY FELINES COYLY WELCOME ALL WITHIN VIEW.

# CONTENTS

# Introduction



MANY TODAY ARE DRAWN TO EASTERN PHILOSOPHIES in their search for inner peace. Similarly, many are drawn to Eastern design because of the sense of harmony and balance that it can impart. *Wabi sabi* (pronounced wah-bee sah-bee) is neither just an excuse for another in the long list of trendy design books based on "Asiatica" nor another variation on Zen-inspired minimalist modernism. It is a system of aesthetic judgement rooted in nature's simple system of order that has long stood the test of time. It embodies concepts that are as fresh today as they were a thousand years ago. Technologies may change, but both nature and basic human needs remain constant. The objective in wabi-sabi-inspired design is to achieve the same sense of ordered placement and balance within interior space that is found within nature.

Wabi sabi is sometimes referred to as Japanese rustic design, but the word "rustic" generally implies crudeness and lack of sophistication. Wabi sabi does not imply crudeness but an earthiness that is the ultimate in sophistication. Moving beyond the glossy, gilded, and gaudy—the simple organic elegance of wabi sabi is for those who have no need to prove who they are. Wabi sabi is for those who are at peace with themselves and want to feel the peace of the natural world around them at all times.

The Japanese sensitivity for creating beauty is legendary. Whether speaking of Japanese interiors with their sparseness, simple but rich palette of organic colors and textures, and consummate manipulation of light and space, or of Japanese gardens with their exquisitely stylized representations of nature, in educated and cultivated circles around the world the Japanese aesthetic sense is considered by many to be the supreme manifestation of sophistication—a paragon of good taste.

In the roughly 150 years since opening its doors from self-imposed isolation, Japan has struggled and striven to embrace all things occidental, modernizing at an unprecedented rate. In the wake of the incoming tidal wave of Western influence, Japan released its own tsunami of influence that continues to sweep across the global community of art and design. The most salient feature of that which distinguishes Japanese design is the spirit of wabi sabi—the very essence of Japanese beauty.



In order to understand wabi sabi, beauty must first be understood on a conceptual level. The traditional Japanese concept of beauty differs radically from that of the West. The Japanese have long held the notion that beauty is not inherent in an object but rather is experiential. Given an ordered set of circumstances, beauty is the elicited response experienced by the perceiver. In other words, beauty is a sensory experience resulting from the process of creating order.

Nowhere in the world has any culture been so prepossessed with the pursuit of beauty as in Japan. The desire to experience beauty has been a virtual national obsession for more than a millennium. Viewed as a vital human need, it has been sought after with the same fervor and energy with which life's staples were pursued. Through this passionate pursuance, the Japanese have achieved depths of understanding beauty scarcely imagined in the West.

Over the course of their long cultural development, the Japanese have come to recognize various levels of beauty. Their conceptualization relegates elaborate ornamentation and vivid color usage to the bottom of taste levels. Obviousness and excess require no real thought or creativity. The highest level of taste moves beyond the usage of brilliant colors and heavy ornamentation to a simple and subdued refinement that is the beauty of *shibumi* (or *shibui*, its adjectival form), which represents the ultimate in good taste through conscious reserve. This is the original "less is more" concept: less color—subdued and elegant usage of color; less clutter—few but perfectly placed furniture pieces and objects in the room, creating a sense of understated refinement and balance. When the beauty of shibumi reaches its highest level of consciousness, it becomes the unassuming elegance of the beauty of wabi sabi.

Although the concepts within wabi sabi are essentially simple, there are depths and nuances of meaning that elude the casual explanation. Wabi is the antithesis of pretension and ostentation. It is the embodiment of humility.

*Wabi* historically meant "wretched, miserable, and forlorn," referring to the dreary state of the human condition. With regards to art and design, it connotes a modesty of choice, a naturalness that is unassuming, referring to austerity of design without severity.

*Sabi*, on the other hand, is spoken of as that which is "mellowed by use, patinated by age, reticent and lacking in the assertiveness of the new." It also means "austere and lonely." Things rusty, worn, or tarnished exhibit the quality of maturity that is sabi. Often referred to as the "bloom of age," it is a quality that can only be achieved through long years of existence. It is neither created nor induced. It simply occurs through the natural process of exposure to the elements or long years of fond usage and the elapse of time. Blue jeans and bomber jackets are two icons of American contemporary culture that possess souls of sabi. The older the denim, the softer and more appealing the jeans become. The more distressed and weathered the leather on a bomber jacket, the more desirability it acquires.



Wabi and sabi have evolved together into an aesthetic that represents the pinnacle of taste, but its purpose is not simply for aesthetic's sake. In our mechanized and computerized lives, it is easy to forget that we are in fact a part of the natural world. The objective behind wabi sabi is to bring us back to our roots, to nature, and to the sense of peace that it can impart to our lives.

THE WARM GLOW OF EVENING'S LAST RAYS CASTS AN ETHEREAL LIGHT ON A GOLDEN BUDDHA FIGURINE. THOUGH SMALL IN ACTUAL SIZE, ITS PRESENCE FILLS A MUCH LARGER SPACE.

## The Spirit of Wabi Sabi

THE SPIRIT OF WABI SABI is based on a simple set of ideals adopted from nature. These ideals are as straightforward as nature itself. It was only through keen powers of observation that the Japanese were able to discern these hidden rules of nature, even though they are simple in their basic concepts. Because they lived as part of nature, they were able to understand it acutely.

A MOTHER AND BABY SEAL APPEAR TO REST ABOVE A FOAMING GREEN SEA IN THIS NATURAL STONE SCULPTURE ENTITLED *SEAL ROCK*.

TEA CEREMONY ACCOUTERMENTS ARE COMPLEMENTED BY THE QUIET BEAUTY OF *TATAMI* MATTING.

From earliest times the Japanese have followed an animistic belief system that deifies all nature. The philosophies of this indigenous religion, Shintoism, have nurtured a deep reverence for all things in the natural order. The Japanese believed that within all things—mountains, rocks, trees, birds, animals, even thunder and wind—dwell the *kami*, the spirits of the divine force. This belief system acknowledges that no life-form and no element is loftier or lowlier than any other. All life has its niche within the grand scheme. Human life is but one small aspect of the natural order. It is no nobler nor more important than any other life-form.

Still, today, rocks are viewed in Japan with the respect that we Westerners reserve for favored family pets. The spirit of wabi sabi implies a modesty of soul that allows one to see and appreciate the nobility in the simple and the common. It seeks to ennoble the ignoble, to take that which convention would consider not worth its focus and place it in a position of supreme importance.

The ubiquitous *tatami*-mat flooring in Japan carries an air of elegance and sophistication, and yet it is woven of rice straw—a discard at the time of harvest. This is a classic example of focusing on beauty in the common, or ennobling the ignoble. The true beauty of the straw is visible because of the

position of dignity in which it is placed. While other cultures quarried marble or felled great trees to make their floors, the Japanese maintained a modesty of heart that enabled them to employ a humbler substance for crafting theirs. The rewards of this choice are many. The rice straw is soft and cushion-like underfoot. It holds insulating qualities that make it warm to walk or sit on. Its delicate yellow color and repetitious woven pattern as well as the quiet beauty of its subtle sheen are unmistakable. The refreshing fragrance of summer grass lingers in the air year-round, and one is constantly reminded of the satisfaction in utilizing an annually renewable resource.

The Japanese have always held a profound belief that their kami would not live in an unclean house. Shintoism is a faith of purification; uncleanness is a form of disorder, and disorder is opposed to all nature.



The concepts behind wabi sabi also owe much to the meditative concepts of Zen Buddhism. The Japanese believe that the moments of embracement by beauty are actually moments of enlightenment, or *satori*. One such enlightenment is that beauty cannot be explained; it can only be experienced.

*IKEBANA*, THE JAPANESE ART OF FLORAL ARRANGING, TRANSLATES PRECISELY IN THE ENGLISH LANGUAGE AS "LIVING FLOWER." THIS ART EXPRESSES THE SPIRIT OF *WABI SABI*, THE VENERATION OF THE ESSENCE OF THE OBJECT.

## BEAUTY OF ALLUSION

The Japanese have traditionally held a moon-viewing in September—not on the evening of the full moon but two nights before. It is called the chestnut moon. Chestnuts are offered and saké is enjoyed, much like during the cherry blossom–viewing in April. The Japanese people have both a preference and a penchant for things imperfect. They find the imperfect not only more alluring but also more poignant. The Japanese believe that the evocative shapes of emerging buds have more ability to touch men's hearts than the glory of the spring tree in full bloom.

Wabi sabi is not found in nature's moments of grandeur or majesty. It is found in meekness. Wabi sabi's jewels must be sought out to be seen. They are found in hidden vignettes, not grand vistas. They are not the obvious. Who would not marvel at the splendor of a spring forest ablaze with rhododendron or azalea blossoms? The very first azalea blossom, however, as it timidly presses open towards the spring sunlight, or the very last blossom as it delicately clings to life, both carry more pathos than the bush in full bloom. "*Mono no Aware*" is a Japanese phrase referring to the ability of an object to move the human heart. Sometimes mono no aware is referred to as the "thusness" or the "ah-ness" of things.

STARK WINTERSCAPE AWAKENS

A LONGING OF THINGS TO COME—

THE BLUSH OF SPRING'S FIRST BLOOM.

A fourteenth-century priest named Kenko wrote of the importance of appreciating imperfection. In his writings he asked, "Is it only when the flowers are in full bloom and when the moon is shining in spotless perfection that we ought to gaze at them?" Do photographers ever photograph the last blossom on the bush? The acknowledgment of the perfection of imperfection is at the very core of wabi sabi. Perfection is a concept, not a reality in a finite world. Within this concept lies the appreciation of the processes of regeneration, which are, in fact, the processes of decay.

No matter its beauty or brilliance, a perfectly full moon creates no energy of anticipation. The perfection of the full moon leaves no room for the imagination to roam. Imperfection involves the viewer in the creative process, because within imperfection is found the allusion of perfection. The full moon is suggested in the moon that has not yet reached its peak, just as the allusion of the full flowering is found within the swelling buds or the falling petals. The images are then perfected in the mind of the observer.

The beauty of allusion, or intimation, is a concept uniquely developed by the Japanese as a natural extension of the beauty of imperfection. The Japanese have understood the power in the indirect conveyance of an idea. They have keenly understood how a fragmentary glimpse stimulates the mind and can, therefore, convey a complete scene more potently than if viewed in its entirety. Even within the spoken Japanese language, the more indirectly a question is answered, the more polite it is construed to be. Because of this, the Japanese have carried the art of circumlocution to heights unimagined anywhere else in the world.

THE SUGGESTION OF AN ANCIENT TREE IS EVIDENT IN BOTH THE ROUGH, ROUND EXTERIOR SHAPE OF THIS UNUSUAL DRUM TEA CHEST, *TAIKO CHA-DANSU*, AND IN THE SINGLE PINE BOW PAINTED ON THE PANEL BEHIND.

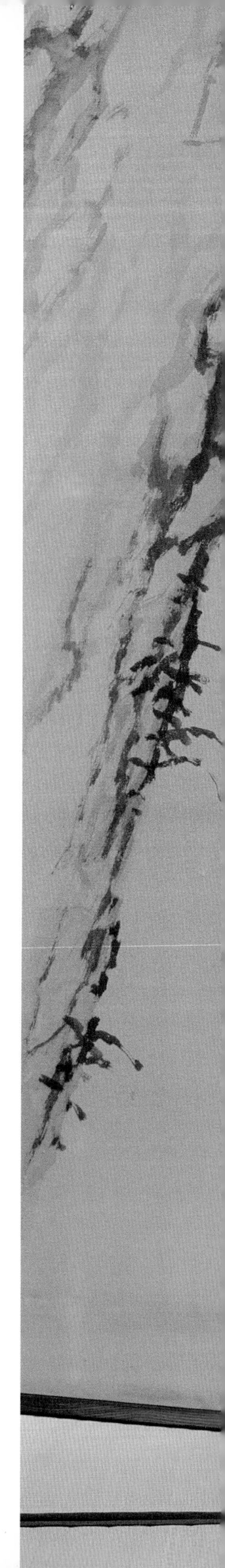

## BEAUTY OF ASYMMETRY

The beauty of imperfection is also admired in nature's aesthetic code of asymmetry. Asymmetry is a sense of balance created without utilizing symmetry. Symmetry, which is a perfection of balance based on an axial model (meaning two equal halves), is a man-made convention. Nature reserves symmetry for living organisms. If symmetry is perfection, then anything less is imperfection. It is in this imperfection of asymmetry that nature organizes its spatial relationships, utilizing randomness and irregularity as the basic components.

A rolling mountain meadow does not have pine trees planted on either side in symmetrically matching rows. Nature does not plant pine trees or any other trees in perfectly straight rows. If the meadow did have matching rows of pines, not only would the rows feel forced but they would appear unnatural. Natural tree-growth patterns are spontaneous and irregular. Creating that same sense of spontaneity, that sense of "everything naturally springing up into its rightful and proper place," is the goal of wabi-sabi-inspired design, which cannot be achieved without understanding the importance of asymmetrical balance.

A relaxed feeling of spontaneity is a key element in the beauty of wabi sabi and shibumi. Interiors based on rigid axial symmetry feel as forced and unnatural as the mountain meadow with perfect rows of trees. The visual boundaries imposed by strict symmetry are rigid and confining. Such boundaries are the antithesis of spontaneity because they look calculated and contrived, because the effort in the creative process shows. Just as in nature, the wabi sabi in objects or in interiors does not show. Because the finished product appears effortless and the skill and the work involved in the creative process is invisible, it feels spontaneous and natural.



SNOW DUSTS A BAMBOO LEAF IN A SIMPLE COMPOSITION OF ASYMMETRICAL BALANCE.

The serene beauty within a traditional Japanese interior has just such an appearance of effortlessness. These interiors have a timeless, even magical feeling that everything is in its perfectly ordered place. The seeming simplicity belies the true complexity of skill and knowledge employed in its creation.



A HORNED CEREMONIAL SAKÉ CASK, CLEVERLY CONVERTED INTO A LAMP, AND A BAMBOO *IKEBANA* BASKET REST ATOP A HALF *MIZUYA-DANSU*, OR KITCHEN CHEST, ATTRACTIVELY USED AS A SOFA TABLE. THE SIMPLE BUT DYNAMIC CHARACTERS ON THE HANGING SCROLL, OR *KAKEJIKU*, EVOKE BLESSINGS OF PEACE AND SAFETY UPON THIS HOME.

## BEAUTY OF IMPERMANENCE

Wabi sabi could be deemed a celebration of sorts of the evanescence of life. It is widely known that *sakura* (cherry blossoms) are the national flowers of Japan. Under ideal conditions their blossoms will last only three days. In stormy weather they may not last a day. The plum, on the other hand, a close relative of the cherry, may bloom for almost a month. So why is the cherry prized more than the plum? The cherry-blossom petals, without so much as a hint of struggle, will release themselves to the most gentle of breezes as if their very purpose is to fall.

IF CHERRY BLOSSOMS IN THEIR PRIDE
COVERED THE FAR-FLUNG MOUNTAINSIDE
DAY AFTER DAY, THE SUMMER THROUGH,
SHOULD WE PRAISE THEM AS WE DO?

— *Anonymous*



The preceding poem is a translation from the *Manyoshu*, the first great Japanese anthology. This collection contained cultured verses that spanned the three hundred years previous to its publication in A.D. 760. While our European ancestors were still tripping about in the Dark Ages, the official governmental Bureau of Poetry in Japan was publishing poetic anthologies. It is evident from the sentiment expressed in this poem that even thirteen hundred years ago the author was contemplating the transient beauty of the sakura.

The cherry blossom, though tinged with a hint of melancholy, is the very symbol of taking joy in life's brevity. As they flutter to the ground, the petals exude the energy of life. It is only logical that those things most elusive become the most prized. Fleeting moments are the most cherished. Wabi sabi is about appreciating the moment, about appreciating the fleeting nature of all life and all existence.

WARM SPRING SUNSHINE SOFTLY ILLUMINATES THE TRANSLUCENT BLOSSOMS OF A WEEPING JAPANESE CHERRY TREE.

Within the moment of creation is felt the first embrace of oblivion. Whether animate or inanimate, the timeless and eternal processes of decay are relentless. There is no stasis in nature. Nature is in a constant state of reclamation. The finest steel can corrode away to a few mere flakes of rust. Granite boulders break down into ever-smaller pieces until they become indistinguishable particles of sand. Wabi sabi seeks to understand and appreciate nature's processes of decay. The spirit of wabi sabi is really a heightened sense of awareness that these are actually processes of maturation and regeneration.

Natural materials and surfaces acquire a sense of dignity and richness through the passage of time. Verdigris, rust, the silvery-gray of weathered wood, and lichens and moss on stone all deserve to be prized as medals of maturity. When we understand the years of exposure to severe conditions required to feather the grain to a delicate texture, we venerate the wood rather than denigrate it. One definition of the word *perfect* is "a state of maturity." Wabi sabi is just such a beauty of maturity. And in the imperfections of maturity, wabi sabi finds perfection.

The wounds, abrasions, scars, and blemishes of long years of use are no less noble than the verdigris or the rust. All things that contribute to the patina of age add character and depth. Wabi sabi is sometimes referred to as "the beauty of eternity" or "the beauty that symbolizes eternity." It is this patina of age that causes us to think of eternity and its timeless processes. It also reminds us of our own vulnerability, that no matter how fleeting life may be, nature itself endures. Nature is permanent and eternal. Perhaps it is this vulnerability at the core of wabi sabi that makes it so appealing.



IRON OBJECTS SUCH AS THIS TEA POT AND THE OPPOSING PAGODA ONLY BECOME MORE APPEALING AS THEY AGE.

## Wabi Sabi Is the Beauty That Symbolizes Eternity

### BEAUTY OF SIMPLICITY

Simplicity is implicit within the concept of restraint. The dictionary defines simplicity as "freedom from ornamentation or absence of deceit; sincerity or unaffectedness." Every word of this definition is potent. Simplicity does not visually, physically, or mentally encumber. It does not pretend to be anything other than what it really is; it is sincere and genuine. Simplicity holds no conceit.

Simplicity of design refers to thoughtfully and consciously limiting one's choices. To limit oneself shows discipline and strength of character. Repetition is a key element of restraint and simplicity. It is concrete proof that choices have been limited.

One can imagine a boulevard lined with trees, each one being a different species—pine, palm, plum, et cetera. Even though there is beauty within each tree, the character of the street feels disjointed and chaotic because of the trees. Now imagine again the same street where all the trees are uniformly tall sweeping ginkgo trees. The feel of the street scene is quite different. It is tranquil and harmonious. The restraint exercised in limiting the choices and the simplicity of repetition in using the single species of tree creates harmony and beauty that far outweigh the disorder created through diversity.

Whether the repetition is of color, texture, or form, it is reassuring. It creates a sense of belonging and naturalness. Just as in nature the repetition of a particular kind of plant growing in a single area says indigenous, so does repetition of design elements create the feeling of belonging within interiors. The reason the pattern of a brick wall is so appealing or a tile floor is attractive is that repetition creates harmony. The same is true of the harmony of colors created through analogous color schemes.

Interiors done in simple, compatible color schemes not only reflect that strength of character, they nurture strength of character. Their simple and tranquil beauty nurtures the soul just as nature itself does. Nature's own palette is repetitious and restrained.

Restraint indicates self-discipline. Nothing is more admirable. The very word evokes feelings of respect and praise. Discipline reflects being in control, and it reflects taking control. Whether an early morning jogging routine or the creation of a serene nature-inspired interior environment, the discipline required is the same. Both require the same state of mind. Both require the strength of mind to resist self-indulgence.

RESTRAINED COLOR SCHEMES, CARRIED EVEN AS FAR AS THE DECORATIVE OBJECTS, CONTRIBUTE TO AN OVERALL FEELING OF TRANQUILITY.

## BEAUTY OF SUBTLETY

As a species, we have moved away from nature. We have moved away from the land and into the concrete canyons of contemporary life. The natural habitat of our food is a slick and shiny supermarket. Microwaves and cellular phones have become life's staples. Where is the poetry in our lives? Where is the subtlety?

No culture in the history of the world has so wholeheartedly embraced such a poetic approach to all aspects of life as the Japanese. Their food, clothing, homes, speech, or even one facet of their lives could not be extricated from this pursuit of beauty. This need for beauty, they feel, runs much deeper than a superficial fix. There is energy in beauty—deep spiritual energy. The fact that beauty is perceived as a vital human need carries great profundity. Possibly they understand something that the rest of the world has not yet grasped. The moment of pause, both immediate and involuntary, that one experiences when embraced by great natural beauty is caused by the recognition of the great sense of balance and order that is beneath all creation.

A MEDITATION LOFT HAS BEEN CREATED FROM AN ATTIC STORAGE SPACE.

Western ideas often resign beauty to the realm of the superfluous. The Japanese perceive beauty as the very essence of life. No people have ever understood the value and importance of restraint and subtlety more than the Japanese. They have been aware of the impact and dynamics of subtlety for at least the past fifteen hundred years, as evidenced by historical writings and by ancient art treasures archived at various sites throughout Japan.

A prime example of the Japanese aesthetic of subtlety and restraint is felt in the art of monochromatic ink painting. It is sheer poetry with a brush. The strength in simple strokes and the depth of suggestion found in the varying grays of the ink are limitless. Though within the musty tones of ink may hide the suggestion of spring's verdure, on the surface it seems to replicate winter's palette of grays.

## WINTER

THOUGH VEILED AMID THESE MISTY SHOWERS OF GRAY,

FUJI IS LOVELIER STILL—UNSEEN TODAY.

—*Basho*



The mere suggestion that Mount Fuji is even lovelier today, invisible because of winter's enshrouding clouds, expresses the true essence of the spirit of wabi sabi. Rather than bemoaning the inability to view the mountain, as would the person who has no poetry in his soul, the beauty of nature's processes is both understood and appreciated.

Winter is the embodiment of wabi sabi. Nature pares down to the bare essentials. Melancholy paints the skies. The very sound of the word *winter*, with its resonant *r*, brings a chill to the mind.

One could begin by taking a walk of discovery. The purpose of this walk is to find all the subtle hidden beauty passed by until now. If perchance it is not presently winter or circumstances do not permit, then a mental walk through a winter woodland will serve the purpose.

A PAIR OF IRON LANTERNS GLOW UNDERNEATH THE EAVES OF THE VERANDAH AS WINTER BLANKETS THE LANDSCAPE IN WHITE.

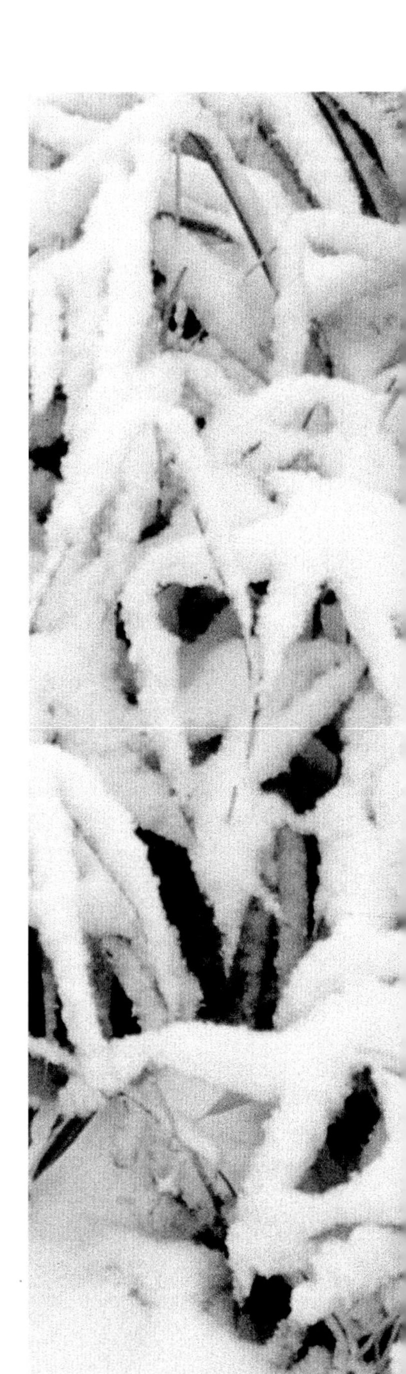

The sparseness of winter allows the true beauty of trees—their growth habits and branching structures—to become defined. Each stark, leafless tree is unique. The varying rich grays and browns of the different tree barks complement the grays of the sky. Some barks have an almost undulating texture.

There is a world of color generally passed right by. These are subtle, rich colors found within the processes of decay. Without the eyes to see them, however, nature's most clever and ingenious contrasts and harmonies will go completely unnoticed.

SNOW-LADEN BAMBOO AND STONE CREATE A MONOCHROME STUDY IN TEXTURE.

THE RUSTY TONES OF
DECAYING FRONDS ARE THE
PERFECT FOIL FOR THE RICH
GREENS OF THE SWORD FERN.

THE SOFT COLOR OF
A DRIED LEAF COMPLEMENTS
THE WET LEAVES BELOW.

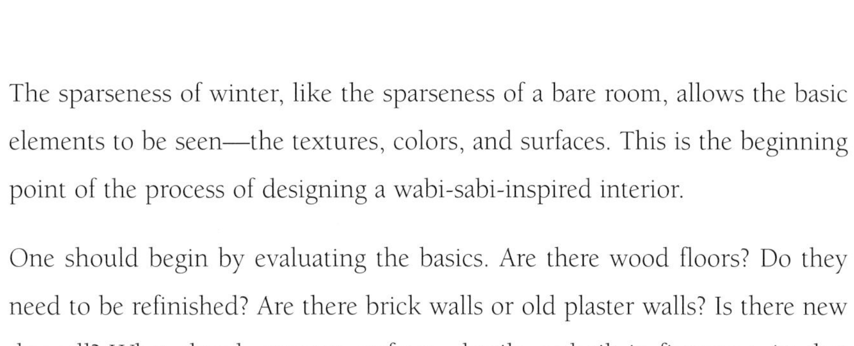

The sparseness of winter, like the sparseness of a bare room, allows the basic elements to be seen—the textures, colors, and surfaces. This is the beginning point of the process of designing a wabi-sabi-inspired interior.

One should begin by evaluating the basics. Are there wood floors? Do they need to be refinished? Are there brick walls or old plaster walls? Is there new drywall? What already present surfaces, details, or built-in fixtures exist that are either desirable or must be changed? Are there elaborate crown moldings? Take a thorough inventory.

After reviewing the basics, the next step is to establish a base color scheme. Look for color and textural clues within the fixtures already present. For example, is there a hearth of brick or stone, and, if so, what colors are in these materials? These clues can be the starting point for the color scheme.

Wabi-sabi colors are always muted—never brilliant or gaudy. The very concept of wabi sabi requires restraint in establishing a color scheme. The more muted the base tones and the more subdued the choice of colors, the more effectively the finished room will quietly restore one's energy. Intense or energetic colors do not restore vitality; they filch it.

However, using muted colors doesn't have to be boring. Many people choose off-white paint for lack of a real understanding of color. They have no idea how much richness a muddy taupe or a dove gray or even a dusty mauve can impart to their room.



THE COLORS OF THE VEGETABLES APPEAR ALL THE MORE BEAUTIFUL AND INTENSE BECAUSE OF THE RESTRAINED COLOR WITHIN THE ROOM.

Wabi colors are usually grayed-down, imperfect versions of original, or base, colors. In mixing color pigment, a process called the pigmentation of opposites—a softened or neutralized version of the original hue—can be achieved by adding some of the exact opposite color to any base hue. These neutralized colors are murky and opaque yet have a richness of pigment. Because of the depth of the actual pigmentation, they absorb more light than basic colors do. It is this ability that gives these colors a feeling of depth. In turn, a tranquil, organic richness is imparted to an interior. The murkier the wall color, the more elegant the finished room will be.

This organic quality is essential to the overall success of a wabi-sabi-inspired interior. The sense of serenity comes in part from the subdued and restrained palette of colors. The pigmentation of opposites gives muted colors a sense of balance and a feeling of timelessness and of permanence.

A NINETEENTH-CENTURY JAPANESE CELADON VASE (ABOVE) ADDS DIGNITY TO THE DINING ROOM BECAUSE OF ITS SUBTLE COLOR AND SIMPLE DESIGN.

A STEEL FIREPLACE CARRIES A RAWNESS THAT ENABLES IT TO WORK WITH ORGANIC ENVIRONMENTS.

## INTIMATE ENCOUNTERS WITH NATURE

A recent national radio commercial for a well-known paint company poked fun at a woman who wanted her walls the same color as the mud puddle in the street in front of her house. This woman obviously has wabi in her soul. Color schemes taken straight from intimate encounters with nature create interiors with the most understated refinement.

The inspiration for the color scheme for an entire house can be found in a single lichen-covered rock discovered on a morning walk. Or it may come from a fleeting moment just after sunset as dusky blues fill the sky with the bloom of night. Nature at her seemingly most insignificant is often at her greatest. Nature's jewels are hidden but can be easily found by those who have eyes to see.

Calming colors—the ones that are restorative by nature—are subdued in tone. Often in nature these colors are found only in decay. Lavender-colored lilac blossoms acquire a brownish-mauve cast as they wilt. When isolated and used in interior settings, this color is rich and appealing. The opaque green of brackish pond water is a particularly pleasing interior wall color. It is literally the color of mountain mud mixed with seaweed, which has been used as wall plaster in traditional Japanese homes for centuries.

THE BEAUTY OF THIS ROOM
IS INSPIRED BY A DRY WINTER
HILLSIDE AT DUSK.

味

A STARK BRANCH SETS A STAGE OF WINTER'S CALMING GRAYS.

WHEN HUMILITY AND HUMBLENESS ARE EMPLOYED, TRUE SOPHISTICATION IS THE RESULT.

Nature is a master colorist. Anything and everything one could possibly want to learn about creating color schemes, color contrasting, and coordination can be gleaned straight from nature itself. This perfection can be seen in many plants—when the color of new leaves contrasts with the mature foliage of the plant or when the color of the blooms becomes a fully realized darker shade of the blush color found at the base of the leaves.

By using clues garnered from the interiors themselves, along with nature's infallible guide, one can choose a master color for a room. Blue, green, coral-rust—any color will work as long as it is muted and subdued. This color will be treated as the base, or main, color throughout the interior. All other colors should play off or against this color.

Black can be an effective accent and ally in outfitting interiors. It does not count as a color because it does not expand a color scheme. It grounds it. Black is technically the absence of color. The absorption of all colors in the light spectrum by the surface pigment allows no light to reflect back and be registered by the eye. On the other hand, white is the presence of all colors within the light spectrum.

THE BLUE DENIM OF THIS CHAIR CREATES A BALANCE WITH CONTRASTING WALLS AND GROUNDING BLACK ACCENTS.

THE MOSSY GREEN OF THESE WALLS (LEFT) SETS A RESTFUL TONE IN THIS BEDROOM.

Even within black there are many variations of warm and cool. Some blacks seem translucent while others seem opaque. The different pigments that are mixed determine the variations. It is the addition of these other pigments that give black a real feeling of depth. One should be cautious not to overuse black. As a rule, it should not be used on a wall but only as a trim or accent. The effect would be counter to wabi-sabi style.

The colors used in the largest ratios must be the most restrained. Restrained refers to the muting or imperfection level of the color. Without this muting, there would be no sense of balance. The larger the surface area to be covered, the greater the restraint there must be with the color. However, restrained does not mean pale. One should not confuse the anemic quality of pastels with the muted depth of wabi-sabi colors.

A JAPANESE ROOT SCULPTURE (ABOVE) IS A PRIME EXAMPLE OF THE ABILITY TO FIND BEAUTY IN THE COMMON.

GOLDEN MUSTARD WALLS IMPART A RICH ORGANIC FEELING TO THIS OFFICE. BLACK ACCENTS DEEPEN THE EFFECT.

Paint colors can be deceiving. What may appear to be a dark paint sample may seem barely darker than white once it is on the walls. Other times, colors may deepen as they reflect off each other. Incorporating gentler, more delicate versions of the same hue nearby can soften stronger colors. A wall color can also be muted by using an overglaze of an opposing color. If a more intense color is chosen for the base wall color, the furniture must be more neutral to balance it.



In small rooms, clever and careful color usage can visually expand the space. Painting two of the walls a different color than the other two walls and the ceiling has the effect of opening up a room.

Too many choices can be burdensome and debilitating, and using a different color in every room creates a choppy effect. One should allow the constraints of wabi sabi to walk him or her through available choices. Analogous colors, or colors with a common base that are closely related, create an instant feeling of harmony. Various colors may be used throughout the home, but they should create a path of colors that are closely related.

## TOUCH OF ASTRINGENCY—THE SIGNATURE OF SHIBUI



Whether color, form, or texture, repeated usage creates a balance and feeling of harmony. It is vital to use restraint in choosing both a color and a textural palette, remembering that balance and harmony are the objectives. Keeping a palette harmonious and simple is not to say that certain complementary and/or contrasting colors cannot be utilized. Within the concept of *shibumi*, the use of an astringent color that both complements and clashes with the base color scheme can be superb.

The word *shibui* actually means "astringent," like the sharp taste of an unripe persimmon. Over the centuries, the word *shibui* has evolved from meaning "an astringent taste" to its current definition: a taste level of astringent-color use that represents the most cultivated sensibilities in the world. As the cornerstone of wabi sabi, the shibui idea of subdued and quietly rich colors overlaps. The signature of this aesthetic is the thoughtful and limited introduction of an astringent color, a color that skews or grates against the base color or colors. The unexpected quality of the seemingly incongruous color creates a dynamic counterpoint. This color must be used sparingly or the effect is lost.

## ECONOMY OF MATERIALS

The concepts originally employed to create Japanese interiors were economy of means and materials. Natural materials used were those most plentifully available without real cost other than the energy and time required to obtain them. Grass-mat floors were woven from the leftover straw after rice harvest. Mud-plaster walls and natural-timber beams were obtained from readily available resources. Seaweed may have been added to the mud to create a rich green tone.

One can find many free materials for wall treatments by using contemporary methods of recycling. Scrap sheet steel with its irregular rust patterns is just one example of material often available at no cost. When applied to walls, it creates an immediate feeling of age and timelessness. Someone in the neighborhood tearing down an old wooden fence might be entreated to allow a neighbor to haul away the weathered fence boards. A weathered wood wall can become the highlight of an entire home and could be available for merely the cost of labor.



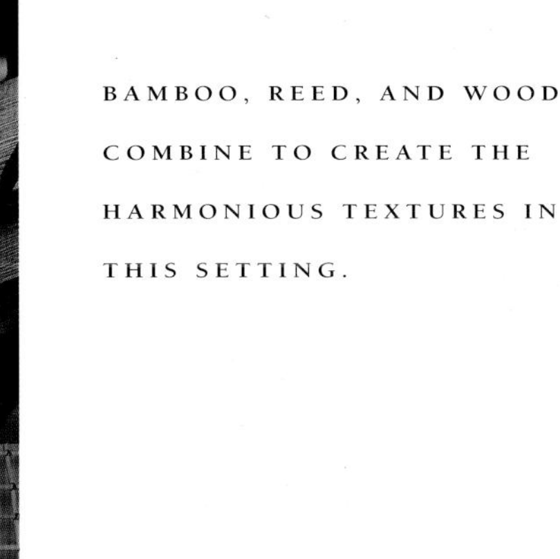

BAMBOO, REED, AND WOOD COMBINE TO CREATE THE HARMONIOUS TEXTURES IN THIS SETTING.

RECLAIMED WOOD AND BRICK (RIGHT) CONTRIBUTE DEPTH AND TEXTURE.

PILLOWS FASHIONED FROM RICE BAGS AND KIMONO SCRAPS PUNCTUATE THIS OUTDOOR GROUPING.

Nature is self-renewing. Fallen leaves become the compost that nurtures next season's growth. Recycling is a basic principle of nature. It is at the heart and spirit of wabi sabi, both in terms of aesthetics and economics. All too often the results of new construction are sterile and uninviting. Using recycled materials can often impart a sense of dignity and maturity that cannot be achieved in any other way.

## Floors and Ceilings

The floor is the foundation of a room. Upon it rests all else, literally and figuratively. Clean simple floors of natural or organic materials are the most appropriate for wabi-sabi interiors. Tile, stone, concrete, cork, bamboo, hardwood—all of these are perfectly acceptable and desirable. If an artificial surface is chosen, organic-looking ones are preferable.

Nothing destroys the potential feeling of peace within a room faster than carpet of intense artificial color. If carpet is chosen for its soundproofing ability, warmth, or other reasons, quiet organic colors should be chosen whenever possible and the pile should be short. Deep pile carpet does not provide a sense of naturalness. It also harbors more dirt.

STAINED CONCRETE FLOOR AND TATAMI RICE-MAT FURNITURE ADD ORGANIC QUALITIES TO THIS MEDIA ROOM.

The goal is to surround oneself with nature, not just objects that remind a person of nature. It is the selection of actual organic surfaces, colors, and materials that create a home within nature, not one protected from it. When inorganic surfaces such as linoleum flooring, Formica, or Corian counters are unavoidable, organic colors or natural-looking patterns should be chosen to avoid jarring the feeling of naturalness within the room.

The principal purpose of a ceiling is to hide the roof. In some types of construction, the ceiling is the roof. The rule with ceilings and with trims on the ceiling (or anywhere else) is to allow them to blend with the walls. Subtlety is the answer. The only purpose of an elaborate crown molding is to draw attention to it. If it is painted the color of the walls and/or ceiling, it will be reduced to textural interest.



THIS ORNAMENTAL *YAHATA*-STYLE CHEST FROM SADO ISLAND DOES NOT APPEAR GAUDY BECAUSE OF THE SIMPLE CHEST CASING AND THE STRAIGHTFORWARD STYLE OF ARCHITECTURE, WHICH ACTS AS A NEUTRAL GROUND.

THE COLOR AND CRINKLED TEXTURE OF A WALL COVERED IN CRAFT PAPER (LEFT) ADD ORGANIC RICHNESS TO A ROOM.

PANELING CUT FROM OLD REDWOOD POLES ALSO IMPARTS AN ORGANIC RICHNESS.

### WALLS

Walls are the single-most dominating feature within an interior space. The color and textural choices for the walls will make or break an interior environment. When choosing wall colors, employ the garden test. Would this color, if painted on a garden wall, look garish and defeat the beauty of the plants in the garden? Would it harmonize if placed next to such natural surfaces as tree bark or rock? If the color is not in harmony with natural surfaces, a more suitable color should be chosen.

天宮

There are many modest organic or organic-looking options for wall treatments: rag-rolled paint over plaster, sponge techniques, crackle-finish paints with glazing, various overglazing techniques, wood, brick, and stone, to name just a few. Using old corrugated tin roofing can give an otherwise ordinary or mundane space an earthy air of sophistication. The effect of any of these methods is a naturalness that makes walls appealing. There are numerous other options. One's imagination is the only limitation.



Modesty does not necessarily refer to cost or economics. There are many costly but modest options. Stone walls in interior settings create a sense of timelessness. Fine cork and grass-cloth wallpapers can instantly create a feeling of organic richness. Some wallpapers covered in real dried leaves are delicate and elegant but unpretentious.

One should not just think color but also texture and tactility as well as tonal expression. It is the polyphony of textures and tones that creates nature's greatest symphonies. In addition, one should be creative, inventive, and, most importantly, confident in choosing modest alternatives. Creating a wall collage of either crinkled pieces of ripped brown-paper sacks or of old newspapers can create a strikingly organic effect. Modesty also refers to color. It refers to subdued organic finishes as opposed to slick brilliantly colored ones that are self-prepossessed. The feeling of organic harmony is the objective.

AN INTRIGUING WALL OF VENT BOARD ALLOWS FOR BOTH PRIVACY AND BEAUTY.

## SPRING

VIOLETS IN RETIREMENT NEAR ITS TRAIL

ARE TOUCHED IN PASSING BY THE PHEASANT'S TAIL.

*—Shushiki*

Wabi sabi in spring is not found in moments of lavish bloom. It is found in hidden jewel-like moments such as the one described above. It is found in the evocative forms of swelling buds and in the flurry of falling petals. In Japan, the traditional new year begins with the spring, when life energies begin to flow again. The energy to start life anew can be found in the simple act of breathing air heavy with the sweet scents of apple blossom and lilac.

Spring is a time of exuberant color and energetic growth. One should not be wooed by nature's springtime extravagance. It is merely a brief aberration of the norm, with the intent of drawing attention to itself for one purpose only—to produce, to ensure the perpetuation of the species. Appreciate and enjoy it for what it is—a seasonal indulgence with a valid purpose behind it.

There is a time and place for exuberant color. Just as nature uses intense color as accents or seasonal splashes, homeowners can also use these accents as seasonal splashes or decorations, not as base colors for a color scheme. Wabi sabi is the beauty of eternity found in the colors of permanence and understatement.

It is important to finalize not only the basic color scheme but also the scheme in coordinating the colors of accessories. The subtle contrast of colors found as new life emerges from winter's dormant buds creates opportunity for many potential color schemes. One should take a springtime walk of discovery, looking for the hidden and the obscure. That is where nature's true gems can be found.

The color pink is generally found as a bloom color in nature, usually in spring or sometimes as the color of winter's blush on a plant. Pink is not usually thought of as a color of permanence or stability. If a person is drawn to the color pink, however, the most elegant and impactive use of pink would be through a restrained presentation. This is done by choosing a neutral base color that is the perfect foil for pink and then playing subtly against it. A muddy taupe, for instance, with a virtually undetectable hint of red in it would set a neutral ground for the pink.

SCATTERED PINK PETALS ACCESSORIZE A DRIED IVY LEAF.

SPRING'S SPLENDOR SURROUNDS AN OLD GRANITE LANTERN.

Another approach would be to use the suggestion of pink found in a dusty mauve with accent touches of pink as delicate as the translucent pink of falling cherry blossoms. Either of these treatments will transcend anything that basic pink walls or pink sofas and a conventional approach to interiors could accomplish.

Just as nature begins to dress itself in spring, so begins the early stages of dress for the wabi-sabi interior, capitalizing on spring's abundant energy. It is here that the task of assembling interior furnishings begins.

THE BACKDROP FOR THE INTERIORS OF THIS SPACE (LEFT) INCORPORATES THE SUGGESTION OF NATURE'S SUBTLE BLOOM IN THE SAME WAY THAT AN EARTHY NINETEENTH-CENTURY SCREEN PROVIDES THE INTERIOR SETTING FOR THIS SIMPLE BURLED ZELKOLVA HIBACHI.

Rugs create softness and warmth underfoot. They help define areas within larger spaces. However, all rooms do not require rugs. If the floor is attractive, why hide it? One might consider the idea of leaving the floor bare for summer and then putting down a rug for autumn as the night air begins to chill. If cold feet are a concern, one can wear slippers, as the Japanese do.

Stay with natural fibers, organic colors, and simple weaves. Coir, jute, sea grass, hemp, rice straw, silk, cotton, and wool rugs all have unique beauty. Patterns and designs within the rug should be subtle and subdued. Carpet roll ends or remnants with the edges stitched to create a finished look can be an attractive alternative. The cost for a remnant is nominal compared to expensive oriental rugs. Cost aside, modesty is the key to creating an interior that has the balance and tranquility of nature.



One should not be locked into the idea that the most expensive option is the best. Just because rugs are expensive, rare, or Oriental does not mean they warrant purchase. Few Oriental rugs are subtle enough to impart a sense of organic harmony to a room. Their elaborate color combinations and intricate patterns draw too much attention to themselves. Generally speaking, their beauty is not a quiet one. Sometimes Orientals with subdued color schemes and subtle designs or patterns can function as a texture in a room. Usually, however, the dynamics of Orientals are too overpowering for the restrained approach of wabi sabi.

In instances where conventional Oriental rugs are used, their boldness must be counterbalanced as much as possible by taking everything else to neutral extremes, or the effect will be lost. Murky taupe-colored walls and sofas can help diffuse the energy of the rug's artificial colors.

DISCIPLINED COLOR CHOICES RESULT IN QUIET TONAL HARMONY.

THE GENTLE ANGULAR LINES OF THE SOFA COMPLEMENT THE STRAIGHT LINES OF OTHER FURNISHINGS.



"MATCHED SETS OF ANYTHING ARE DOUBTLESS THE WORK OF THOSE WHO HAVE BUT LITTLE TASTE: ''TIS BETTER TO HAVE DISSIMILARITY.'"

—*Kenko*

Early in the fourteenth century, Kenko wrote these inspired words—words that are still as accurate today as they were seven hundred years ago. The idea that matched sets are unattractive stems from the lack of imagination and serendipity involved in their creation or assemblage. Matched sets, like perfect symmetry, are the expected.

Kenko also wrote of how it is preferable to have things that are old rather than new. He expressed how the craftsmanship of former times was waning. Times may change, but the basic human experience remains the same. Even today, quite often the craftsmanship of older furnishings exceeds the quality of current pieces.

One must always keep furnishings in proportion to the space they are to fill. Large rooms do require some oversized pieces. Bigger rooms also need to be broken down into groupings or intimate settings to reduce the space to human dimensions. A homeowner must also be careful not to clutter a room with too many small pieces of furniture unless the uniformity of design contributes to a larger sense of harmony.

Smaller rooms usually require smaller-scale pieces. However, sometimes the most efficient use of space within a small room is to have a single large sofa hugging the wall or even wrapping around a corner.



INTERESTING AND IRREGULAR SHAPES IN BOTH FURNISHINGS AND APPOINTMENTS ADD DIMENSION TO INTERIORS.

While imagining a room in its finished state, one should carefully consider the first images that come to mind. To what extent is the room furnished with tight symmetry? What can be done to break it up? Now, the arranger should imagine the room again based on the asymmetrical setup. Is it more interesting this way?

Tight symmetry, unless broken at some point by a touch of asymmetry, holds the mind hostage. Some examples of breaking symmetry while using matching end tables would be to use different lamps on each table or to place a lamp on only one of the tables. Another option would be to have matching lamps on mismatched end tables. The challenge in trying to achieve a balance in wabi-sabi interiors is to know exactly where the perfect point of balance lies between repetition and asymmetry.

Matching sofas opposing each other can be an efficient usage of space in accommodating seating needs. However, to maintain a sense of wabi sabi, the axial symmetry created by the two sofas facing each other needs to be broken either by art objects on the mantel or with other furniture pieces, such as chairs, occasional tables, or lamps.

Convention would say to echo the symmetry of the matching sofas by putting either a mirror or a painting above the mantel with matching candlesticks on either side. This arrangement is neither interesting nor attractive. It is merely conventional. The room feels staged with this setup. To lose some of the staginess, one might move the mirror slightly to one side and then place both candlesticks together off to the other side. If needed, a small, unobtrusive art object may be placed just to the mirror side of the candlesticks for balance and counterpoint. The asymmetry now created above the mantel can balance the symmetry of the opposing sofas and make them appear more attractive.



The placement of major furnishings will either create or break the flow of energy within a room. One should not place furniture pieces in obstructive positions or place them in ways that impede the natural flow of traffic into and out of a room. When entering a seating area, if the approach feels uncomfortable, the alignment of the furniture needs to be altered.

THE GOLDEN TONES OF THE FURNISHINGS FOIL THE INTENSITY OF THE BLUE WALL.

宇 治
茶
舗

Sometimes the simple act of angling a major piece of furniture can make all the difference. Angling a focal point, such as an armoire, across a corner softens a room that may otherwise feel boxy. Slightly angling a sofa whose back faces the entrance of a room can visually break the feeling of obstruction and allow a gentler flow, or approach, into the room.



One principal difference between Western and Japanese design concepts is that Japanese design focuses at the center of a room or space and works its way outward; most Western design concepts begin with the walls or outer perimeters of the space and work inward. If one stands in the center of the room and works outward, he or she may be surprised at how different the results might be. Sofas need not be glued to the walls.

CREATIVITY, IMAGINATION, AND SERENDIPITY SHOULD BE EMPLOYED WHEN CHOOSING FURNISHINGS.

Many styles of Japanese cabinetry are said to resemble American Shaker design because of their supremely simple lines. Known and admired around the world, the Japanese *tansu* is a storage cabinet whose beauty is simply born of function. The word *tansu*, which means "wooden cabinet" or "chest," is pronounced *dansu* when used in compounds. For example, the word for tea in Japanese is *cha*, so a tea tansu is a *cha-dansu*.

THE JAPANESE INGENIOUSLY DESIGNED STAIRWAY CHESTS, *KAIDAN-DANSU*, THAT SERVED BOTH AS STEPS AND AS SPECIFIC STORAGE SPACES.

THE SIMPLICITY OF TANSU DESIGN ALLOWS FOR THE USAGE OF VARIOUS STYLES IN THE SAME SETTING.

歡喜天宮

Tansu are essentially square boxes outfitted with various drawers and doors designed to give the utmost in utility and permanence. The range of uses for tansu is broad. Some were merchants' chests used for the storage of ledgers, and some were apothecary chests to house herbal remedies. Others were clothing, tea, kitchen, and sea chests. Wherever there was a need, a cabinet was developed to accommodate that need. The common element between them was a practical approach to both design and construction.

Most design features are strictly function-related. Iron fittings and straps reinforce joints and stress points that could weaken over time through use. Sliding doors instead of hinged doors effortlessly lift out for better accessibility to the contents inside. Asymmetry is often utilized in the construction of Japanese furniture. The small drawers that give tansu an asymmetrical balance are born of the need for spaces to store small items. Often left in a raw state with just the subtle sheen of natural wood for a finish, the pieces gradually acquire a natural patina through years of service. These cabinets are as functional today as when they were built. Their beauty is in their utility as well as their design.

A strict code of simplicity does not mean that certain pieces of furniture cannot have any ornamentation, but the more restrained the design, the more impact the end result will have. One piece with exaggerated ornamentation that draws too much attention to itself will destroy the effect. Simple design should be the focus.

THIS STRIKING *ISSHO-DANSU*, OR CLOTHING CHEST, NOW HOUSES LINENS AND TABLEWARES.

THESE TABLES ENHANCE THEIR INTERIOR ENVIRONMENTS WITHOUT DRAWING ATTENTION AWAY FROM OTHER POINTS OF INTEREST WITHIN THE ROOMS.

## TABLES AND DESKS

Attractive tables of simple design are available but they may have to be actively sought to be found. A table should have no hidden agenda of adding ornamentation to a room. Whether a dining table, cocktail table, or an end table, the piece should have straightforward appeal.

A DESK MADE FROM AN OLD RAIN-SHUTTER DOOR IMPARTS A FEELING OF ELEGANCE AND DIGNITY TO AN OFFICE SETTING.

Again, one need not be trapped by convention. A distinctive and intriguing option for tables of all kinds is to use old architectural pieces like doors or window grilles and have them made into tables with steel bases. The steel can be enameled black or even acid-treated to give it a feeling of wabi sabi. This can create a tone within a room that is simply unmatched by commercially available pieces. The goal is to create an unconventional interior, so an unconventional treatment is required.

Traditional desks are heavy in both appearance and actual weight. The purpose of their design is to accommodate stuffy offices where the concept of less is more has not yet been discovered. Sleek computer desks with designs of merit have recently appeared on the market. Though their designs hold promise, most are slick laminate with no hint of natural materials. A simple wooden table would make a desk that is more wabi sabi. One should ask the question: What is a desk? What are the bare essentials? The answer is a work surface with drawers. Only convention says that both the work surface and the drawers have to be parts of the same piece of furniture.

The one thing a bed must be is comfortable. Whether the sleeping surface is placed directly on the floor, on a metal frame, or on a custom-made wooden platform, the most important characteristic of a bed is its ability to allow a restful sleep. However, the design of the bed is what will make or break the bedroom aesthetically.

A headboard visually grounds the bed to the wall so the bed does not feel like it is floating in the room. It also gives back support when the bed is occupied, and it protects the wall. Keeping that in mind, one can be creative with the headboard but not overly ornamental. A treatment as simple as a piece of plywood covered with foam rubber and then with muslin stretched neatly over it can be attractive and comfortable.



Antique architectural elements, such as transoms and doors, offer interesting possibilities. If time and money allow, the pursuit or creation of something original that will specifically suit one's needs can be satisfying. But one should

THE TEXTURES IN THIS BEDROOM EXEMPLIFY THE CONCEPTS BEHIND WABI SABI—ORGANIC AUSTERITY OF DESIGN WITHOUT SEVERITY.

THE ART OF OGATA KENZAN
JAPAN'S GOLDEN AGE Momoyama
THE HERITAGE OF JAPANESE ART
ART OF THE LOTUS SUTRA

be leery of premade beds with footboards because they tend to isolate a bed within a room. The visual and literal barrier created by the footboard can disrupt a room's flow of energy by chopping the sleeping area into a confining cubicle.

A bedcover need not be expensive or even an actual bedcover to be attractive. A bedspread can be as simple as an inexpensive cotton throw and still look great. Texture is important. The natural nubbiness of certain weaves imparts a richness of texture as it complements the earthy color chosen for the walls. When selecting bedcovers, linens, and towels, it's best to stay away from floral or geometric patterns. Wabi sabi lends itself to natural fibers and subdued earth colors.



WHETHER CUSTOM OR CONVENTIONAL, A BED CAN BE AS UNIQUE AS ONE WISHES.

Utility and simplicity are the key words. Beware of billowing draperies dragging the floor. This is not to say that drapes or other fabric window treatments cannot be attractive choices for window dressings, but it is important to analyze exactly what is needed from them.

The two utilitarian purposes of window treatments are privacy and sun protection. Less is more when it comes to windows, since allowing the outdoors in as much as possible is what most people prefer. Where the view is particularly appealing and privacy is not an issue, windows can be left bare. This expands the interior space by visually pulling in the outside. Where some privacy is required, plants work in lieu of window treatments. Substantially sized plants with an architectural look can be attractive and create a visual barrier. But one should avoid clusters of little insignificant plants. They contribute to a feeling of clutter.



Another option worth considering is that of freestanding screens placed in front of windows. The fact that they are removable allows unsurpassed versatility. Again, stay with organic materials and simple construction so as not to draw undue attention to the screen. The quiet richness of woven organic materials will add more to the overall beauty of a room than the most expensive Chinese *coromandel* screen. Remember that price is not the determinant of beauty.

SIMPLE ORGANIC TEXTURES AND COLORS INVOKE A RESTFUL FEELING.

If window dressings are to be used, those constructed of natural materials are the best choices. Many attractive options will contribute to a sense of organic harmony. Blinds made of split bamboo, reed, or other organic fibers will lend a touch of grace through the delicate way they filter sunlight. Their airiness also helps a room feel less boxed in.

Simple cloth blinds, such as Roman shades, can also work well, so long as they are natural-looking fabrics of restful organic colors. One should refrain from fabric colors with any eye-catching appeal on window treatments unless the wall is the same color. If the wall is the same color, then the fabric color of the blind or curtain creates harmony.

The curtain design should be as simple as possible. The simpler the curtain, the more effective it will be. Curtains made with fabric tabs instead of hooks or loops, like Japanese *noren* curtains, carry an aura of quiet sophistication. One should use organic-looking fabric without bold patterns. Subtle tone-on-tone patterns that create a feeling of texture are fine. Slubby fabrics, fabrics with nubby irregular threads, give a hand-woven feel because of their imperfections and are particularly desirable.

IN THE TRADITIONAL JAPANESE CULTURE, ATTACHMENT TO NATURE WAS SO COMPLETE THAT A HOUSE WAS NOT CONSIDERED A HOME WITHOUT THE INCLUSION OF A GARDEN. WHEREVER POSSIBLE, ONE SHOULD ALLOW THE OUTSIDE TO COME IN.

GREENE & GREENE: MASTERWORKS

Café curtains or half-window shutters give privacy where needed without closing off a room to natural light. Wooden slat shades or plantation shutters can work as well. Wherever possible, it is best to avoid using metal or plastic Venetian blinds. If metal blinds are unavoidable, make sure that their color is subtle and harmonious with the wall color. Regardless of the kind of window treatment chosen, it is the actual organic surfaces and textures that infuse a room with a feeling of natural harmony. The objective of creating a subtle harmony of colors and textures should be foremost in one's mind.

While on the subject of windows and curtains, it is appropriate to briefly address closet treatment. One can approach the opening to a closet the same as he or she would a window. A closed closet door boxes in a room the same way a boarded-up window would. Closet curtains are an age-old option that is scarcely considered any more. Not only can they be more interesting than basic closet doors, but the texture both softens a room and expands its visual space because of the lack of a solid wall. Freestanding screens, the same kinds used at the windows, are another viable option. The important idea to remember is to not be stuck in the rut of convention.

## Summer

A MOONLIT EVENING: HERE BESIDE THE POOL,



STRIPPED TO THE WAIST, A SNAIL ENJOYS THE COOL.

—*Issa*

This haiku portrays a classic sentiment—finding beauty and dignity in the otherwise lowly and insignificant. The haiku form of poetry originally evolved as a praise-nature song. It became the recognized form for both verbal and written expression of moments of enlightenment, or *satori*. This haiku is just such a moment. Issa may have sat with his own garments stripped to the waist because of the heat, then, noticing the snail, realized a moment of satori.

A simple basket filled with summer grasses and hung on a wall in the entryway can be an elegant and easy way to set the tone of the season for the entire house. Traditional Japanese houses have a *genkan*, or entry vestibule, where the shoes are removed before stepping up into the home. Within the genkan, a counter-like display surface for floral arrangements is standard. Upon entry, guests are greeted by an appropriate seasonal tribute. A shoe repository, or shoebox, as the Japanese call it, is usually cleverly hidden below the floral-display surface.

FRUITS OF THE SEASON, JAPANESE PEARS, ECHO THE FAWN COLOR OF SUMMER GRASSES SEEN UPON THE MOUNTAIN THROUGH THE TREES.

Few Western homes have an entry vestibule, but a similar area is provided by either an entry hall or the suggestion of an entry vestibule. If a home is lacking an entry hall, one can be created by placing a screen or barrier to give a sense of passage into the home. Seasonal tributes are just as effective when a screen is used to emulate an entry hall.

Just as the garden comes into full dress in summer, so, too, will the interior begin to find its full dress. But it is best not to create too many high points of interest within any room. Wabi sabi is about purposeful placement, resulting in a balance that unfetters and frees the psyche. One should be thoughtful and restrained in selecting decorative pieces.

By their very nature as a light source, lamps emit a jewel-like attraction that draws the eye. As such, extreme care should be taken in their selection. Lamps take on one of two personalities within a room. Either they are utilitarian and nondescript, functioning strictly as light sources, or they are ornamental, becoming objects of focus. In order to function in the utilitarian category, they must be ultimately simple. This does not mean they have no sense of design; this merely means they do not possess extra ornamentation. It is their simplicity that allows them not to draw focus.

On the other hand, lamps of unique character must be placed with the same care and understanding as key objects of focus. An object of focus is any object other than furniture considered worthy enough to be used as a decorative furnishing. These can include but are not limited to photographs, paintings, ceramic vases, sculpture, candlesticks, pottery, and baskets. The designation "objects of focus" does not mean objects that scream for attention. It refers to objects with soul and hidden meaning that cause one to pause to contemplate them—hence the term "object of focus."



THE SIMPLE ADDITION OF BLUE SOFA PILLOWS FOR THE SEASON CONTRIBUTES TO AN OVERALL FEELING OF SUMMER FRESHNESS.

When searching for lamps, one should consider utility—whether one is looking for an accent light to illuminate a dark corner or a reading lamp beside the bed. The scale of the space where the lamp is to be placed should also be considered. The lamp's surfaces are equally important and need to be considered as well. Slick, glossy, and shiny are the antithesis of subdued and unassuming. It is best to choose lamps with dignified design but quiet appeal.

Gentle touches of light throughout the home can create a tranquil feeling of meditation. For this reason, one should never settle for any new lamp available commercially. If the "perfect" lamp proves elusive, searchers should remember that creating a wabi-sabi interior is a process, not a quick fix.

A TRADITIONAL JAPANESE WOODEN LANTERN CHOSEN FOR ITS ARTISTIC MERIT ILLUMINATES AN EARLY-TWENTIETH-CENTURY CLAY DOLL.

Objects of utilitarian usage that have been converted into lamps often make the most intriguing ones. Their shapes and unique characteristics born of specific function give them a sense of purpose. Old candlesticks, baskets, jugs, and urns have soul and, when tastefully converted into lamps, give character to a room unequaled by lamps generally available to consumers.

Lamps should be interesting without being overly assertive. They should be allowed to carry their space without overdressing the surface around them. One should resist putting too many objects around the base of the lamp. Because of the spotlighted effect that any object receives when placed within the lamp's immediate glow, any feeling of clutter transfers to the entire room. The care with which lamps are chosen and placed is as critical to the overall sense of harmony as any other single element.

Convention demands that pictures, paintings, and photographs be placed on every available wall space no matter how small. Wabi sabi requires that this convention be broken. First, one must refrain from filling every inch of wall space. Instead, a person should thoughtfully choose those spaces that are key to creating a feeling of balance within a room and dress those. Second, one should not be locked into the mind-set of using only conventional art as objects of focus on walls or elsewhere. Wabi sabi does allow conventional art, but simply asks not to resign oneself to the limits of convention.

The more open wall space within a room, the more spacious the room will seem and the more important the decorative objects placed within the room will seem. The reason objects in museums appear to be so important is that they are presented in a light of singular importance. The space around them allows them to be focused upon without distraction. This same concept should be considered when choosing any objects of focus.

BARE WALLS ALLOW ARCHITECTURE AND FURNISHINGS TO FUNCTION AS ART.

Hallway walls do not require art. Art on walls in narrow passageways not only breaks up the already limited space and makes it feel even more cramped and confined, but it creates visual obstructions that impede the sense of flow through a house. When dealing with hallways, especially narrow ones, one must allow them to be just passageways. Even long spacious halls do not warrant art in every available space. The simple act of not hanging pictures up and down hallways speaks volumes about the taste level of the home's occupants. The dignity that this single act of restraint can impart to a home cannot be emphasized enough.

天神地祇八百萬神
神祇官統領神祇伯王

千萬両
宇治
茶
橋本茶舗

Undecorated spaces in a room contribute to an overall feeling of openness and spontaneity. This concept can be observed in nature—in how the forest is best appreciated by viewing it with the meadows surrounding it. Just as meadows act as a counterpoint to wooded areas and subliminally give space for the forest to continue to grow, the open spaces left in rooms also subliminally give the sense that the rooms still have space for new growth.

One should not cover walls with snapshots but instead take up scrapbooking. Scrapbooking gives purpose and place to those boxes of old photos and keeps one from feeling the need to pin them up. It creates order from chaos. Scrapbooks can then be kept neatly stored away.

Objects placed on walls right next to windows distract the eye from traveling through the window to the outside. They contribute to a feeling of being boxed in by drawing attention to the wall. Particular attention must be given to these spaces so as not to overdress them. Usually the window itself and the window treatment perform the function of dressing exterior walls, with the exception of large expanses where there are no windows. The window is ornament enough for exterior walls. The focus should be on directing the eye outward if the view is attractive. Even if there is no significant or worthy view beyond, the importance of the window as a light source needs to be recognized. The way to not diminish a window's importance is to underdress the wall space around it.

## ACCESSORIES AND APPOINTMENTS—OBJECTS OF FOCUS

The spirit of wabi sabi requires that nothing be overemphasized. This means that art objects of focus be approached thoughtfully, keeping in mind the idea of creating an overall sense of harmony. Instead of choosing objects simply for their outward appeal, it's best to break from convention, choosing objects that have character and meaning.

Within the masterful handicrafts and folk art of Japan lies an entire world of exquisite objects that exhibit just such hidden meaning and character. One example is the unpretentious beauty of Japanese pottery, revered the world over. Equally renowned is the subtlety and refinement in Japanese basketry.

FOLK ART OBJECTS, LIKE THESE FESTIVAL DOLLS AND THIS STRAW RAINCOAT, BRING A SENSE OF HUMBLE DIGNITY WHEN USED AS OBJECTS OF FOCUS.

The very term *folk art,* as opposed to high art, implies modesty. Folk art objects are handcrafted of natural materials for utility's sake. Their beauty stems not from conscious artistic effort but from the beauty of the natural materials used coupled with the skill acquired through long years of practice. The objects of focus need not be of Japanese origin. Objects that resonate with the spirit of wabi sabi can be found in indigenous cultures around the world. Implicit is the skill and unpretentious artistry in the craft and the earthiness of the natural materials used in its creation.

IN THE TRUE SPIRIT OF WABI SABI, NATURE VENERATES THIS BARNACLE-ENCRUSTED CLAY VESSEL ONCE USED AS AN OCTOPUS TRAP.



One should consider hanging antique textile pieces or architectural fragments on walls. These objects with a former life have depth to their existence. They have soul. Old wooden drying racks, window grilles, or other lovingly crafted objects of utility—when placed purposefully—take on a sophistication and poignancy where their sense of value and importance far exceeds their actual worth. Just the breach of convention in placing an object of humble beginnings in a position of importance imparts a feeling of richness and dignity that no form of opulence can produce.

## THE FAMILY ALTAR

The mantel in a conventional Western home assumes somewhat the same position or place as the *tokonoma* in a traditional Japanese home. The tokonoma is the distinctive art alcove that is the main focus of the living room where guests are received. This art alcove is where the family's most treasured possessions are displayed on a rotating basis—paintings, vases, sculpture, even an heirloom suit of armor.

Not only is the mantel the most conspicuous and prominent feature in the Western living room but Westerners have a tendency to place their most prized possessions either above it or on it. It is the closest thing within our culture to a family altar. The one major difference between the Western mantel and the tokonoma is that the mantel is not viewed as a place for rotating art the way the tokonoma is. Generally, a prized object is placed on the mantel and left there forever, often acquiring more clutter around it with every year that passes.

THE FEATHERED GRAIN AND SOFT COLOR OF A SIMPLE BARN-WOOD FRAME COMPLEMENTS THE DELICATE TEXTURE AND SUBTLE TREATMENT OF THIS LOVELY IMAGE.

One should avoid a cluttered mantel at all costs. It sets the wrong precedent for the entire house. The dressing of the mantel should be approached with an air of reverence. The mantel surface is the single-most-important surface in the house. It carries great symbolic weight as well as visual weight because of its prominence. Thoughtfully choosing an object or objects that express not only who the homeowner is but also what the home's aesthetics are, best expresses wabi sabi.

Wabi sabi encompasses an almost childlike fascination with the natural world. This idealism allows one to delight in anything and everything, from the subtle color change of a wet rock to a twisted piece of driftwood. Humility of heart brings modesty of choice. Can anything be more beautiful than the fragile and humble beauty of a bird's nest?



Whether just a branch of winter hawthorn berries or a bowl of pinecones, objects of focus should include items straight from nature. They have a way of validating everything else around them. The Japanese have created an entire art form around this idea of bringing little tidbits of nature inside. It is called *ikebana*, the Japanese art of flower arranging.

## OVERDRESSING A ROOM

The concept of not filling every available bit of space also holds true for flat surfaces such as tabletops. If every level surface in a room has objects on it, the room will feel cluttered. The serenity and fluidness of wabi sabi are then lost to self-indulgence. One should resist the temptation to fill every space, whether it is a wall or another flat surface.

The temptation to overdress a room is virtually irresistible. A room can only handle so many high points of interest before the look of not knowing when to stop becomes apparent. The problem with this look is that it is apparent to everyone but the one who created it. The fine line between tastefully done and overdone is almost indistinguishable. The line can be crossed over without so much as a hint of notice. Once overdressing a room begins, there is no stopping the insidious clutter.



IMPORTANT OBJECTS, LIKE THIS NINETEENTH-CENTURY TEA-LEAF STORAGE VESSEL THAT STILL CARRIES ITS ORIGINAL RICE-STRAW LID, NEED TO BE PRESENTED WITH SINGULAR IMPORTANCE.

Once any space becomes overdressed and clutter finds a foothold in a corner of a home, then the clutter-breeds-clutter syndrome begins to take over. In order to compete, every other space screams for occupancy. Right before one's very eyes, clutter eventually fills every available surface.

Restraint and reserve are the cure and the antidote to clutter. The only way to protect oneself is to prepare the mind in advance to say no. It is both gauche and ostentatious to display at once every art object one possesses. Having a limited selection of tasteful items on display is the answer. The Japanese have done this for centuries.

A COLLECTION OF FOUND OBJECTS IS CAREFULLY DISPLAYED WITHOUT DETRACTING FROM THE IMPORTANCE OF OTHER OBJECTS, SUCH AS THIS PAIR OF NINETEENTH-CENTURY CLOTHING CHESTS.

## AUTUMN

SCATTERED WITH MAPLE LEAVES WHERE NO ONE STEPPED

MY GARDEN PATH IS BETTER LEFT UNSWEPT.

— *Hekigodo*



No garden path in autumn is properly dressed without fallen leaves. Nature's ever-changing brocade finds ever-more-glorious patterns to weave in her last moments.

Just as summer has lulled us into a false sense of security that its languid days will last forever, along comes the first frost of fall. One should set aside time to enjoy an autumn walk of discovery, savoring the earthy aroma of wet leaves underfoot and the sweet scent of ripening grapes.

One should study the color patterns of turning leaves, noticing how an entire side of one tree may turn red while the other side fades to yellow. Collected cattails and bulrushes growing alongside a country road or an inner-city canal can be placed in and around the home to create an air of seasonal awareness. If one cures the cattails in a mixture of equal parts shellac and turpentine, they won't explode or pop.

Autumn is a time of year to enjoy the fruits of one's labors. It is time to organize and plan the rotation of seasonal displays and decorations. If homeowners have a garden, they can time the pruning of deciduous shrubbery and trees that are particularly colorful in fall. These branches can be trimmed and taken inside for all to enjoy the fullest advantage of the seasonal splendor.

DRESSED FOR FALL, THIS ROOM NOW EMBRACES THE COLORS OF THE SEASON WITH A CHANGE OF ART AND TEXTILES.

Autumn is also a time for self-improvement. It is the perfect time to study the art of ikebana, using the garden's gleanings to make seasonal arrangements that express individuality. Or one can study poetry, such as the Japanese haiku.

A time for reflection and assessment, it is the ideal time to decide to what extent one's home interior has met one's expectations. Is the home overly decorated to the point that this goal is defeated? Are feelings of quiet natural harmony imparted?

THE SPIRIT OF WABI SABI ALLOWS THE BEAUTY OF ALL SEASONS TO BE CAPTURED, AS WITH THESE PERSIMMON-COLORED WALLS, WHICH WILL EXPRESS AUTUMNAL WARMTH YEAR-ROUND.

## THE ACT OF LIVING VERSUS THE ART OF LIVING



It would appear upon entering a traditional Japanese home that the Japanese are the least materially oriented people in the world, that consumerism has not yet reached their shores. However, in keeping with the spirit of wabi sabi, objects in a traditional house are kept tucked away until the moment of need. In traditional homes, an adjacent storage building called a *kura* is used for rotating the family collection of art objects and off-season clothing. In many smaller homes or apartments, a single room is often set aside for storage space.

Life begets clutter, clutter that requires constant editing. One should not fall into the trap of keeping things just for the sake of keeping them. If an object has sincere meaning, merit, or honest utility, it should be kept. But the end goal is to create an environment that unfetters the mind as well as the home. The only way to achieve this is to pare down.

A TRADITIONAL *GETA BAKO*, OR SHOE CHEST, NEATLY STORES GARDEN CLOGS, RUNNING SHOES, AND HIKING BOOTS OUTSIDE THE KITCHEN DOOR, LEAVING THE DUST OF THE WORLD OUTSIDE.



Wabi sabi should be valued in conduct and character as well as in inanimate objects. One of the key purposes of the tea ceremony is to cultivate such character traits as modesty and restraint. Wabi sabi can be seen even as a way of life—a way of looking at and appreciating the world and a way of finding inner peace by keeping in tune with natural rhythms and appreciating the subtleties that slip past in the hurried pace of our high-tech world. Giving pause to appreciate the majesty of a pinecone can help give balance to an otherwise hurried mind.

Wabi sabi is not for everyone. Some people are unable to let go of their bold floral prints, gilded mirrors, and silk flowers. The lack of wabi in their souls will not allow them to grasp the power and strength of simplicity. One of Albert Einstein's most inspired bits of wisdom was "The masses are always deceived." This is the source of fads and the reason people wear clothing that is unflattering to their physiques. This is also the source of conventional norms of interior design.

The spirit of wabi sabi gives one the eyes to view life from a more poetic approach. Just as poetry has rules and limiting conventions, so wabi sabi has its parameters and limiting conventions. It is these very restrictions and self-imposed restraints that give one the freedom necessary to create. It seems like a paradox, but it is only within boundaries that freedom truly exists.

No culture in the history of the world has so wholeheartedly embraced such a poetic approach to all aspects of life as the Japanese culture. Neither their food, clothing, homes, nor speech—not one facet of their lives—can be extricated from this pursuit of beauty. This need for beauty runs much deeper than a superficial fix. Beauty has energy—deep spiritual energy. The fact that beauty is perceived as a vital human need in Japanese culture carries great profundity. Possibly the Japanese understand something that the rest of the world has not quite grasped. The moment of pause that one experiences when embraced by great natural beauty is both immediate and involuntary. Western ideas often resign beauty to the realm of the superfluous. The Japanese perceive beauty as the very essence of life.

**Arise Gallery**
6925 Willow Street NW
Washington, DC 20012
(202) 291-0770

**Asian Antiques**
199 Stockbridge Road (Route 7)
Great Barrington, MA 01253
(413) 528-5091

**Asiatica**
4824 Rainbow Boulevard
Westwood, KS 66205
(913) 831-0831

**Brookside Antiques**
6219 Oak Street
Kansas City, MO 64113
(816) 444-4774

**Decoro**
224 East Ontario Street
& 2000 West Carroll Street
Chicago, IL 60611
(312) 850-9260

**East & Beyond Ltd.**
6727 Curran Street
McLean, VA 22101
(703) 448-8200

**Gallerie Tansu**
1622a Sherbrooke West
Montreal, Quebec H3H 1C9
Canada
(514) 846-1039

**Garakuta-Do**
580 North Nimitz Highway
Honolulu, HI 96817
(808) 524-7755

**Genji**
Japan Center, Suite 190
22 Peace Plaza
San Francisco, CA 94115
(415) 931-1616

**Honeychurch Antiques Ltd.**
1008 James Street
Seattle, WA 98104
(206) 622-1225

**Japanache**
146 North Robertson Boulevard
Los Angeles, CA 90048
(310) 657-0155

**Kagedo**
520 First Avenue South
Seattle, WA 98104
(206) 467-9077

**Kotani Oriental Antiques**
324 East Lane Street
Raleigh, NC 27601
(919) 856-0508

**Lotus Gallery**
1019 East 2100 South
Salt Lake City, UT 84102
(801) 467-6662

**Lyric Japanese Antiques**
8705 Fifth Avenue NW
Seattle, WA 98107
(206) 782-4062

**McMullen's Japanese Antiques**
3172 Bunsen Avenue
Ventura, CA 93303
(805) 644-5234

**Miyamoto Japanese Antiques**
25 Madison Street
Sag Harbor, NY 11963
(516) 725-2192

**Nakura Inc.**
110 West Harris Avenue
South San Francisco, CA 94080
(415) 588-6115

**Narumi Japanese Antiques**
1902 B Fillmore Street
San Francisco, CA 94115
(415) 346-8629

**Old Japan, Inc.**
382 Bleecker Street
New York, NY 10014
(212) 633-0922

**Shogun's Gallery**
206 Northwest 23rd Avenue
Portland, OR 97210
(503) 224-0328

**Silk Road Gallery**
131 Post Road East
Westport, CT 06880
(203) 221-9099

**Tansuya Corporation**
159 Mercer Street
New York, NY 10012
(212) 966-1782

**Three Cranes Gallery**
82 South Main Street
New Hope, PA 18938
(215) 862-5626

**A Touch of the Orient**
Garrett Snuff Mills
Yorklyn, DE 19736
(302) 239-3626

**Warren Imports**
1910 South Coast Highway
Laguna Beach, CA 92651
(714) 494-6505

**Yoshino Japanese Antiques**
104 East Colorado Boulevard
Pasadena, CA 91105
(818) 356-0588

**The Zentner Collection**
5757 Landregan Street
Emeryville, CA 94608
(510) 653-5181

## Photographic Credits

**James Crowley:** Photo opposite introduction page, 2–3, 6, 11, 13, 23, 24, 38, 40, 41, 42, 48, 61, 70, 72, 73, 107, 108, 109, 114, 135, 136, 138, 142, and 146.

**Brian Griffin:** Title page, 21, 63, 64, 98, and 102–3.

Pages 44, 45, 46, and 47 were photographed in collaboration with **Marilyn Lewis Interiors.**

All other photographs in the book are by **Joseph Putnam.**

*A sincere thanks to all those who graciously opened their homes*

*A special thanks to John and Bobbie McMullen*